Charlotte Brontë

the novelist's visits to
Bridlington, Scarborough, Filey
and Hornsea

Kevin Berry

Highgate Publications (Beverley) Limited, 1990

Principal sources:

Charlotte Brontë: The Evolution of Genius — Winifred Gérin, 1967.
The Life of Charlotte Brontë — Mrs E.C. Gaskell, 1857.
A Guide to Filey and Scarborough — E.W. Prichard, 1853
The Brontës: Their lives, friendships and correspondence, 1932

Acknowledgements:

The Brontë Society, for access to the Parsonage Library.
Kathryn White, of the Parsonage Library, for advice and help.
John Markham, for patience and encouragement.

Illustrations:

Grateful thanks are due to the following for permission to reproduce illustrations:
Bayle Museum Trustees
Mark Beever
Brontë Society
Mrs Christine Clubley
Humberside Libraries
Martyn Kirby
North Yorkshire County Library

British Library Cataloguing in Publication Data

Berry, Kevin
  Charlotte Brontë at the seaside: the novelist's visits to Bridlington, Scarborough,
  Filey and Hornsea.
  1. Fiction in English. Brontë, Charlotte, 1816-1855
  I. Title
  823.8

ISBN 0-948929-39-1

Published by Highgate Publications (Beverley) Ltd.
24 Wylies Road, Beverley, HU17 7AP
Telephone (0482) 866826

Printed and Typeset in 10 on 11pt Plantin by
B.A. Press, 2-4 Newbegin, Lairgate, Beverley, HU17 8EG
Telephone (0482) 882232

ISBN 0-948929-39-1

Cover picture: Bridlington, 1848.
(*Reproduced by permission of Humberside Libraries from the collections in the Beverley Library*)

Charlotte Brontë.

Priory Church, Bridlington, as it was in Charlotte Brontë's time, before the western towers were added.
(*Reproduced by permission of Humberside Libraries from the collections in the Beverley Library*)

Bridlington Quay from the Pier.
(*Reproduced by permission of Humberside Libraries from the collections in the Beverley Library*)

4

INTRODUCTION

Stark and tragic, years of sadness and illness brightened all too briefly by astonishing literary success. The life of Charlotte Brontë has become steeped in popular images of a gloomy and introverted family living in seclusion in their drab parsonage on the edge of a windswept moor.

It is not an entirely accurate picture but Charlotte certainly knew more than her share of sadness. When only eight years old she was sent away to the Clergy Daughters' School at Cowan Bridge near Kirby Lonsdale. Her sisters, Maria and Elizabeth, were already there, but within a few months Maria was dead from consumption and Elizabeth died soon after, her already frail body ravaged by fever. Charlotte loathed her time at Cowan Bridge; she always blamed neglect and ill treatment at the school for both tragedies and, not surprisingly, her harrowing experiences were used to vivid effect when describing the dreadful Lowood School in her novel, *Jane Eyre*.

Charlotte, Emily and Anne each had books published in the year 1847 — *Jane Eyre*, *Wuthering Heights* and *Agnes Grey* respectively. Then, within the space of nine months, Charlotte had to bury her brother, Branwell, watch her sister, Emily, fade away and die and then take the terminally ill Anne on a long and difficult journey to Scarborough for a last glimpse of the sea. Within three days of their arrival Anne was dead.

After the funeral Charlotte made the necessary arrangements for a headstone and then left Scarborough. She travelled a few miles south to Filey where she stayed for a week, taking some comfort from the calm and seclusion of what was then a tiny fishing village. Charlotte loved the sea. She was always, throughout her life, entranced and excited by the power and majesty of crashing waves and wide windswept horizons. Friends remembered her being rendered speechless and she was often moved to tears.

Her first real holiday had been spent near Bridlington, or Burlington as it was then called. The chance to get away from Haworth had come at a time in Charlotte's life when she was overwhelmed with feelings of dread and hopelessness and could only despair for the future. Bridlington lifted her spirits and brightened her outlook; she had anticipated the sea with joy and her hopes had been fulfilled. Charlotte would never forget the happiness and excitement of that first visit. Indeed, when the Brontë sisters were at a later date contemplating setting up their own school, Charlotte at first suggested Burlington as a likely location, but the idea came to nothing.

After the tremendous success of *Jane Eyre* Charlotte was bombarded with the inevitable invitations to stay with the wealthy and the famous. She was always reluctant to leave her father but consented to go to London, Manchester and Edinburgh, and stay in country houses in Lancashire and the Lake District. Once away from the shelter of her home, she was the centre of curious attention, an uncomfortable feeling for a shy and awkward young woman. In London she was treated as something of a celebrity, moving in fashionable social circles and meeting such literary luminaries as Thackeray and Harriet Martineau.

Even in Haworth and the neighbourhood of Keighley some knew the secret of her pen name. She was the celebrated and perhaps even notorious writer, Currer Bell, and the church sexton made many a shilling pointing her out to visitors.

At various times in her life Charlotte went to Bridlington, Scarborough, Filey and Hornsea. Her days spent on the Yorkshire coast were an escape from times of devastating depression and a relief from the anxieties of her writing. Charlotte could wander narrow streets and follow cliff top paths alone and unnoticed. She could hide from the world.

The landlady at her Filey lodgings, a Mrs Smith, did not discover until many years later just who her quietly spoken guest had been...

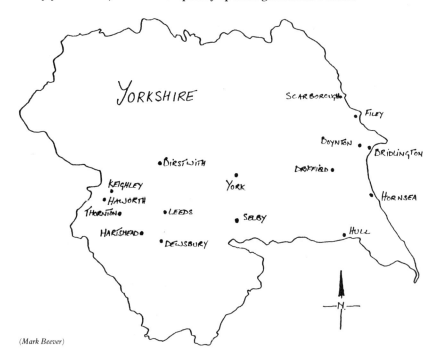

(*Mark Beever*)

Section One

BRIDLINGTON, SEPTEMBER 1839

'A theme of pleasant recollection'

Cleethorpes, or Cleathorpe as it was then known, was the first suggestion for a seaside holiday. Charlotte's close friend, Ellen Nussey, had planned to travel to the coast for health reasons and she suggested that Charlotte should go with her, having realised from her letters that Charlotte was in a state of deep depression.

Charlotte needed a holiday. She had endured three months of tedium and torment as a governess with the Sidgwick family of Stonegappe, near Lothersdale. Her misery, homesickness and longing for both escape and security were apparent in a desperate letter written home to her sister Emily:

'Write whenever you can, I could like to be at home, I could like to work in a mill, I could like to feel mental liberty, I could like this weight of restraint to be taken off. But the holidays will come.'

In her letters to Ellen Nussey Charlotte complained at some length of having 'a set of pampered, spoilt, turbulent children, whom I was expected constantly to amuse as well as to instruct' and her utter dejection was quite obvious: 'at times I felt — and, I suppose seemed — depressed'.

She was certainly in low spirits, but blame could not be entirely attached to Mrs Sidgwick or her brood, spoilt or otherwise. Charlotte admitted that her mistress was considered to be an agreeable woman who was always cheerful but Charlotte absolutely loathed the long hours with the children and the endless evenings spent with a heap of the family's needlework on her knees. She was deeply shy, she looked dowdy, and she was never in sparkling health. Rather than venture into the drawing room for a pen, and so risk having to speak to a house guest, she chose to write many of her letters in pencil.

Charlotte was simply not governess material, she expected help and sympathy from Mrs Sidgwick, but none came.

'To my astonishment I was taken to task on the subject by Mrs Sidgwick with a stress of manner and a harshness of language scarcely credible. Like a fool, I cried most bitterly, I could not help it — my spirits failed me at first. I thought I had done my best — strained every nerve to please her — and to be treated in that way merely because I was shy and sometimes melancholy was too bad.'

When Charlotte eventually returned to Haworth in July her relief was evident. She wrote to Ellen Nussey — 'I left Stonegappe a week since, I never was so glad to get out of a house in my life...'

She had failed as a governess, perhaps the only means of employment open to a young woman in her situation. Charlotte was ambitious, she wanted to make something of herself, but the future was beginning to look both bleak and daunting, devoid of both pattern and purpose. The joy of being back home with her family would lift her spirits but only temporarily. Charlotte needed a complete break, a complete change of scene, and she was almost wild with excitement when Ellen suggested a holiday by the sea. But would she be allowed to go ? Would her father give his consent?

'Your proposal has driven me "clean daft" — if you don't understand that ladylike expression, you must ask me what it means when I see you. The fact is, an excursion with you anywhere — whether to Cleathorpe or Canada, just by ourselves, would be to me most delightful. I should, indeed, like to go; but I can't get leave of absence for longer than a week, and I'm afraid that would not suit you — must I then give it up entirely? I feel as if I could not; I never had such a chance of enjoyment before; I do want to see you and talk to you, and be with you. When did you wish to go? Could I meet you at Leeds?'

A *p.s.* was added to the letter telling of a sudden change in Charlotte's mood:

'Since writing the above, I find that aunt and papa have determined to go to Liverpool for a fortnight, and take us all with them. It is stipulated, however, that I should give up the Cleathorpe scheme. I yield reluctantly.'

Both Rev Patrick Brontë and Aunt Branwell had wanted to reject the scheme immediately; their suggestion of taking the family to Liverpool was a hasty compromise, a sudden whim of an idea to take Charlotte's mind off the seaside. Her father was greatly concerned that two young women should even consider travelling so far without the benefit and protection of a chaperone. He refused Charlotte's pleadings but Charlotte persisted.

A letter to Ellen, dated 4 August, was more hopeful:

'The Liverpool journey is yet a matter of talk, a sort of castle in the air; but, between you and me, I fancy it is very doubtful whether it will ever assume a more solid shape. Aunt — like many other elderly people — likes to talk of such things; but when it comes to putting them into actual execution, she rather falls off. Such being the case, I think you and I had better adhere to our first plan of going somewhere together independently of other people. I have got leave to accompany you for a week — at the utmost a fortnight — but no more. Where do you wish to go? Burlington, I should think, from what Mary says, would be as eligible a place as any. When do you set off? Arrange all these things according to your convenience; I shall start no objections. The idea of seeing the sea – of being near it — watching its changes by sunrise, sunset, moonlight, and noonday — in calm, perhaps in storm — fills and satisfies my mind. I shall be discontented at nothing.'

The suggestion of Burlington/Bridlington had come from Mary Taylor, a friend of both Charlotte and Ellen. The three girls had met when they were pupils at Roe Head School, Miss Wooler's establishment near Dewsbury.

Ten days later Charlotte's resolve had begun to weaken. The one and only gig available for hire in Haworth was over at Harrogate for an indefinite period. She suggested walking part of the way to Ellen's home at Birstwith but Patrick Brontë would have none of it. Aunt Branwell was making plain her worries about the weather, the roads and the four winds of heaven — in fact any potential calamity she could think of:

'I grieve that I should have so inconvenienced you; but I need not talk of either Friday or Saturday now, for I rather imagine there is small chance of my ever going at all. The elders of the house have never cordially acquiesced in the measure; and now that impediments seem to start up at every step, opposition grows more open ... Reckon on me no more; leave me out in your calculations ...'

Ellen Nussey reasoned that the only thing to do was to go to Haworth ready and prepared for a holiday as if she fully expected Charlotte to be ready and waiting. When she arrived in her brother Henry's carriage Patrick Brontë and Aunt Branwell were almost too surprised to raise any objection. Charlotte hurriedly packed her things and in no time at all she was waving from the carriage as it clattered off.

Apart from providing the necessary transport for the first stage of the journey, Henry Nussey had made some other arrangements but had kept them secret. He had been the curate at Burton Agnes, just six miles inland from Burlington, and he still had friends in the neighbourhood. He had written to them when Burlington had first been suggested for the holiday, the thought of Charlotte and Ellen's care and protection seemingly uppermost in his mind. Henry Nussey had known Charlotte for many years, in fact he had proposed to her earlier in the year. Charlotte had flatly, though kindly, refused him and many Brontë scholars have since suggested that Henry Nussey was the model for St John Rivers, the rather dull clergyman/missionary who unsuccessfully courted Jane Eyre.

The girls journeyed to Leeds station and from there Charlotte and Ellen had their first ever train ride as far as Selby. Railway lines had not then been laid any further so they had to go on to York by coach and thence to Driffield. Many other travellers were going in the same direction and there was a scramble for seats at York, the two girls being forced to continue their travels in an open 'fly'. Fortunately for them the weather was rather pleasant and as a consequence the journey proved quite enjoyable.

At Driffield's Bell Hotel a Mr John Hudson was waiting for the York coach, expecting Charlotte and Ellen to be on it. He was a gentleman farmer, living with his wife at Easton House Farm which was just two miles

Market Place, Driffield. Bell Hotel on right.   (Mrs Christine Clubley)

from Burlington. He was a great friend of Henry Nussey and the two men had arranged that the girls would be taken by Mr Hudson to stay at Easton. Charlotte and Ellen had planned to take lodgings at Burlington Quay but Mr Hudson was rather shocked, considering the waterfront not quite suitable for two respectable young ladies. When the coach pulled up without Charlotte and Ellen, the anxious Mr Hudson had made a post-chaise available for them and had directed the innkeeper to send the girls out to Easton when they eventually arrived.

Mr and Mrs Hudson insisted that the girls should stay at Easton House for the duration of their holiday and their holiday was to last a month, decisions certainly made with the full backing of Patrick Brontë and the Nussey parents. Charlotte could not hide her disappointment. Easton House was surrounded by grassy slopes, and views of the sea were restricted to distant patches of grey and blue.

Ellen remembered:
'Whenever the sound of the sea reached her ears in the grounds around the house wherein she was captive, her spirit longed to rush away and be close to it.'

Easton House, reproduction of a watercolour by Charlotte Brontë.

They could have caught a glimpse of the sea by climbing hills but a glimpse was not enough for Charlotte. She would not look, she wanted her first sighting to be especially memorable. 'Don't tell me any more,' she told Ellen. 'Let me wait.'

She waited until the third day of their captivity and then the two girls sneaked off to follow the Gypsey Race, a stream that has its source near Boynton and flows by what was the Hudsons' land eventually to reach the sea at Bridlington's harbour.

When the girls were close enough to appreciate the wide sweep of the sea Charlotte was suddenly overcome with emotion, overwhelmed by the power and beauty of what she saw. Her favourite poems and paintings had excited her imagination and she was not to be disappointed.

Ellen, the ever considerate and supportive friend, wisely walked a little further on to leave Charlotte alone with her thoughts:

'She was quite overpowered … she could not speak till she had shed some tears … Her eyes were red and swollen, she was still trembling … for the remainder of the day she was very quiet, subdued and exhausted …'

Burlington was a town of two quite distinct settlements. The Quay, where the girls had first planned to lodge, was a cluster of inns and alleyways and fishermen's cottages. Some way inland was 'Old Burlington', the sedate houses and shops of Westgate and the High Street leading to the Bayle and the majestic Priory Church of St Mary.

11

It was and still is essentially Georgian in character with some elegant Regency details. There are fine bow windows, pillared doorways and a refreshing neatness in the warm brickwork and rooflines. Thankfully there has been little change, the narrow streets are now tarmac instead of cobble

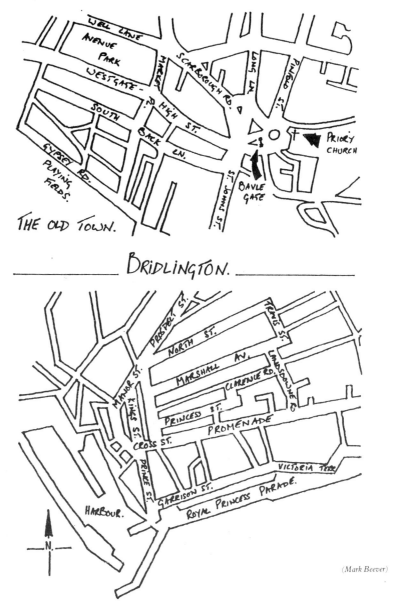

THE OLD TOWN.

BRIDLINGTON.

(Mark Beever)

and cars drive along them, but this little piece of Bridlington is so very quiet, even on the busiest of bank holidays.

'When I was a girl I went to Bretton about twice a year, and well I liked the visit. The house and its inmates specially suited me. The large peaceful rooms, the well-arranged furniture, the clear wide windows, the balcony outside, looking down on a fine antique street, where Sundays and holidays seemed always to abide — so quiet was its atmosphere, so clean its pavement — these things pleased me well.'

The quotation comes from Charlotte's fourth and last novel, *Villette* (1853), the first part of which is set in the 'clean and ancient town of Bretton', a description supposedly inspired by her impressions of Old Burlington.

When Charlotte and Ellen returned from their clandestine walk to the harbour there was no censure from the Hudsons and the two friends were mightily relieved. They could now walk to the sea whenever they wanted, their time at Easton House was to be enjoyed ... walks in the woods at Boynton, rambles on Wolds pathways, exploring the delights of Burton Agnes and going again and again to the seashore.

Easton House had been built in 1810. It was long and low, white-washed and red-tiled with a porch and trellis work covered in a mix of honeysuckle, wild rose and rampant ivy — a vivid enough contrast to Haworth parsonage. Charlotte spent an afternoon painting a picture of the house, and a black and

East Field Farm, 1990. (Martyn Kirby)

13

white copy of her watercolour, with Mr and Mrs Hudson in the background, can be seen in the Bayle Museum.

Another exhibit is a Regency seat for two persons from Easton House ; it has a book box that was said to have been fitted for Charlotte's benefit.

Unfortunately Easton House was demolished in 1961, though not without protest, to be replaced by strictly functional buildings of harsh red brick and corrugated steel with the new name of East Field Farm. The handful of other farmhouses nearby give some indication of what Easton House must have looked like.

To find East Field Farm take the B1253 Easton Road, now also known as the York Scenic Route, out of Bridlington to the scattered hamlet of Easton. Where the open fields begin, the farm can be found at the roadside on the left.

John and Sophia Hudson were a delightful and kind couple. What made Charlotte feel even better was the company of her hosts' seven-year-old niece, Fanny Whipp, who would eventually be adopted by the childless Hudsons. Charlotte and Ellen were captivated by the little girl and she certainly must have been a charmer because Charlotte, by her own admission, had little experience of likeable children. Little Fanny was affectionally nicknamed 'Hancheone', a German term of affection, by Charlotte and much of the youngster's looks and personality can be found in the character of Pauline Mary in *Villette*.

Charlotte and Ellen were at Easton House for almost three weeks and then Mr and Mrs Hudson suggested that the girls could take lodgings at a house they knew of near the Quay. Charlotte was surprised and overjoyed.

It was perhaps during the commotion of packing her belongings that she mislaid her wire-rimmed spectacles, a loss mentioned by many biographers who have given the impression that Charlotte could not have seen the sea properly on her first walk to the harbour.

She wrote to Ellen after the holiday: 'Did you chance, in your letter to Mr Hudson, to mention my spectacles? I am sadly inconvenienced by the want of them. I can neither read, write, nor draw with comfort in their absence, I hope Madame won't refuse to give them up.'

'Madame' could have been a reference to the landlady of the house at the Quay.

The Hudsons were kind and generous. They visited the girls each day with baskets of fresh provisions from their farm, a kindness appreciated even more when Charlotte and Ellen realised that between them their resources could just about manage a week's rent with a little left over for the journey home.

Their lodgings were at a house on what is now known as the Esplanade. It is difficult to place the house with a great degree of accuracy but it did look out onto the sea and was quite close to a Methodist chapel known to locals as the 'ranters' chapel' because of the din and commotion coming from it.

14

Seat from Easton House in Bayle Museum, Bridlington. (*Bayle Museum Trustees*)

Charlotte loved looking out to sea and walking on the long stretches of sand. Ellen recalled in later years how the antics of holidaymakers would often amuse her friend, especially the evening promenade on the nearby pier when the elegantly dressed ladies and gentlemen did not so much walk as shuffle, such was the great press of people wanting to see and be seen.

Charlotte's enthusiasm and spirit might have dimmed with the traumas of the following years but she always treasured the memory of her holiday at Burlington.

A letter to Ellen Nussey, dated 24 October 1839, vividly described her delight and left no doubt that the holiday had refreshed and invigorated her:

'Have you forgotten the sea by this time? Is it grown dim in your mind? Or still can you see it, — dark blue, and green, and foam-white; and hear it roughly when the wind is high, or rushing softly when it is calm? ... I am as well as need be, and very fat. I think of Easton very often, and of worthy Mr Hudson, and his kind-hearted helpmate, and of our pleasant walks to Harlequin Wood, to Boynton, our merry evenings, our romps with little Hancheone, etc., etc. If we both live, this period of our lives will long be a theme of pleasant recollection ...'

Writing to Henry Nussey, four days later, Charlotte tried to be more restrained but could not hide her joy:

15

'I will not tell you of what I thought of the sea, because I should fall into my besetting sin of enthusiasm. I may, however, say that its glories, changes, its ebb and flow, the sound of its restless waves, formed a subject for contemplation that never wearied either the eye, the ear, or the mind.'

Another letter to Ellen, written all of six years later, contained a fond and eloquent reference to that first holiday:

'Remember me very kindly to Mrs Hudson ... Tell her that our stay at Easton is one of the pleasant recollections of my life — one of the greenspots that I look back on with real pleasure.'

Charlotte would return to the sea and to Easton and the Hudsons many years later, seeking solitude and comfort after the most tragic months of her life.

Entrance to Bridlington Harbour, c.1870.

(*Reproduced by permission of Humberside Libraries from the collections in the Beverley Library*)

SCARBOROUGH, MAY 1849

'Charlotte, you must bear up, I shall sink if you fail me.'

Branwell Brontë had died in September of the previous year. Emily caught a chill at his funeral, her condition worsened almost daily and she died in December. Even before the old year was out Charlotte had noticed, with a feeling of grim foreboding, that Anne was visibly ailing.

In January, 1849, a doctor was sent for, Mr Teale, a lung specialist from Leeds, and his diagnosis of Anne's condition amounted to a death sentence. Patrick Brontë was devastated, he sat on the couch beside his daughter, hugged her to him and just whispered, 'My dear little Anne!'

Her decline was chronicled in the frequent letters Charlotte wrote to Ellen Nussey:

10 January — 'Anne had a very tolerable day yesterday, and a pretty quiet night last night, though she did not sleep much.'

15 January — 'Her cough is the most troublesome at night, but it is still rarely violent. The pain in her arm still disturbs her.'

22 January — '... today she looks very pale and languid again. She perseveres with the cod-liver oil, but still finds it nauseous.'

11 February — 'I hope the respirator will be useful to Anne, in case she should ever be well enough to go out again.'

16 March — '... her cough is at time very hard and painful, and her strength rather diminished than improved.'

24 March — ' May God support her and all of us through the trial of lingering sickness, and aid her in the last hour.'

Anne lingered until May. She bore her suffering with a characteristic patience and submitted passively to a number of painful and uncomfortable treatments — blisters, carbonate of iron, cod-liver oil and hydropathy. Charlotte and her father had resigned themselves to the inevitable, and Anne must have known what was going to happen. They retained a semblance of hope, but each in their own way was prepared for yet another tragedy. Their words of optimism were futile, but hope kept them going and they would rather hope than give way to despair.

Charlotte had obviously been unable to continue her writing during the sad winter months. She had been preparing the manuscript of *Shirley*, a novel requiring much research, but Anne's quiet undemanding nature

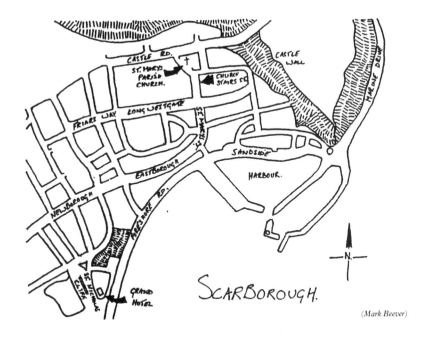

SCARBOROUGH.

allowed Charlotte sufficient time to finish the second volume and send it off to Smith, Elder and Co, her publishers.

In a letter to Ellen Nussey Charlotte said: 'Her illness has none of the fearful, rapid symptoms which appalled in Emily's case. Her mind seems generally serene and her sufferings hitherto are nothing like Emily's.'

Then Anne began to talk of the sea, mentioning Scarborough in particular. She begged to be taken there. She clung to a belief that the sea air might in some way improve her health, or at least that is what she told Charlotte and Ellen. Many Brontë authorities have mentioned the hope of a miracle sea-cure but it is more probable that Anne had calmly pondered over what was going to happen and had concluded that it would be better if she was away from Haworth.

Perhaps Anne wanted to spare her father yet more anguish. The parsonage had already witnessed two deaths, the couch in the dining room was a constant reminder of Emily's last days and Mr Brontë still slept in the room where Branwell had died. Poignant reminders were everywhere.

Anne had lived away from Haworth for more than four years, working as a governess with Mrs Robinson of Thorpe Green Hall, Little Ouseburn, a village near York. She had in a very real sense created a life and identity away from the family home and it must be acknowledged that she was the only one of the Brontë offspring to make a success of regular employment.

With the Robinsons she had spent many summer days in Scarborough and the town had become her favourite place.

Her novel, *Agnes Grey*, carries vivid descriptions of a bustling seaside town and the inspiration is unmistakable:

'There was a feeling of freshness and vigour in the very streets; and when I got free of the town, when my foot was on the sands and my face towards the broad, bright bay, no language can describe the effect of the deep,clear azure of the sky and ocean, the bright morning sunshine on the semicircular barrier of craggy cliffs surmounted by green swelling hills, and on the smooth, wide sands, and the low rocks out at sea — looking, with their clothing of weeds and moss, like little grass-grown islands — and above all, on the brilliant, sparkling waves. And then, the unspeakable purity and freshness of the air!'

Anne was anxious to make arrangements for the journey, offering to pay all the travelling and lodging expenses from a small legacy left by her godmother. In April she suggested that Ellen accompany her, reasoning that Charlotte would be better off at the parsonage, relieved of her nursing duties and able to look after their father. The suggestion caused a further delay. Charlotte contacted Ellen and made known her objections. She could not impose her sister, who was weakening daily, on a friend, not even so close a friend as Ellen. Taking Anne all the way to Scarborough was just too onerous a task for one person.

There were further delays, many of them no doubt deliberate, but Anne was quietly persistent. Medical and family opinion insisted on waiting for more agreeable weather but when the warmer days arrived Anne could hardly walk unaided. In late May she finally overcame all objections and the necessary arrangements were made.

Ellen Nussey had been told to meet the sisters at Leeds station on Wednesday, 23 May, but Anne's departure had to be delayed until the next day. There was no way of letting poor Ellen know of the change of plan and as a consequence she wasted many hours at the station before making up her mind to go to Haworth and find out what was happening. During her long wait Ellen had watched two trains arriving at the platform where she expected to meet Charlotte and Anne; from each of the trains a coffin was taken to a waiting hearse.

On the Thursday Ellen left Haworth parsonage with Charlotte and Anne. They changed trains at Leeds and broke their journey to York, Anne being so weak that she had to be carried across platforms. They stayed at the George Hotel, an old and busy coaching inn, which was in Whip-ma-Whop-ma-Gate, the city's shortest street. The site of the hotel is now occupied by a building society office and a small paved area with seats.

Anne's spirits revived a little after a shopping spree for bonnets. She enjoyed being taken to York Minster, remembering the many times she had been there with the Robinson family. Ellen watched her marvelling at that splendid building and heard her murmur — 'If finite power can do this, what is the ...?' But the thought died on Anne's lips.

On the Friday they arrived in Scarborough. Charlotte's friend, Miss Wooler, had taken a house in the North Bay and had offered accommodation, but Charlotte, all too well aware of the inevitable outcome of their journey, had preferred a lodging house. The three young women took rooms at No 2 The Cliff on St Nicholas Cliff where Anne had often stayed with the Robinsons, a plain house on the site now occupied by the familiar outline of the Grand Hotel. The hotel was built in 1867 and a plaque on the wall by the main entrance commemorates the Brontë link.

Next day the three girls went out on to the beach to be driven in donkey carts. They stayed for about an hour and Ellen later recalled that Anne was concerned because her boy driver was forcing his donkey to too great a speed. She insisted that he stop and then took the reins herself.

On the Sunday Anne hoped to go to morning service but her companions thought the effort would be too much. Later in the day she managed a short walk to the beach and then sat down on a nearby bench to watch Charlotte and Ellen.

There was a glorious sunset to be enjoyed from their large sitting room window. Ellen described it:

'The evening closed in the most glorious sunset I ever witnessed. The castle on the cliff stood in proud glory, gilded by the rays of the declining sun. The distant ships glittered like burnished gold ; the little boats near the

Plaque on Grand Hotel, Scarborough. *(Martyn Kirby)*

beach heaved on the ebbing tide, inviting occupants. The view was grand beyond description. Anne was drawn in her easy chair to the window, to enjoy the scene with us. Her face became illuminated almost as much as the glorious scene she gazed upon.'

Anne then talked to Charlotte at some length. She spoke of the wisdom of returning home, perhaps now coming to realize that Charlotte would have too much of a burden if forced to return home with a coffin.

Anne seemed calm in the morning. Then at eleven o'clock she felt a sudden change in her condition and a doctor was sent for. Anne asked him if there was time to reach home alive but he was not hopeful, and when she pressed him to speak the truth he admitted that her life would be at an end within hours.

She died at two o'clock, quietly and peacefully.

Charlotte decided that Anne should be buried at Scarborough. Anne had wished it so and there was the desire to spare Patrick Brontë a third funeral. Charlotte and Ellen chose a plot in the east yard of St Mary's Church on Castle Hill overlooking the South Bay. It was where Anne had placed the proposal scene in Agnes Grey :

'... I shall never forget that glorious summer evening, and always remember with delight that steep hill, and the edge of the precipice where we stood together, watching the splendid sunset mirrored in the restless world of waters at our feet ...'

The funeral service had to be held at Christ Church on Vernon Road because St Mary's Church was undergoing restoration work. Christ Church, which no longer exists, was on a site now occupied by a supermarket next to Scarborough Library.

The service was held on Wednesday, 30 May. There were three mourners — Charlotte and Ellen and a lady holidaymaker from Birstall. Mention has often been been made of the lady but she has not been named; given that Miss Wooler was in Scarborough, it is most probable that it was she.

Charlotte was close to exhaustion. Her father wrote urging her to stay longer at the seaside.

She did, and the ever loyal Ellen stayed with her. Their rooms had been reserved until 7 June and after that date Charlotte and Ellen journeyed a few miles south to find Filey.

Letters to W S Williams, a reader at her publishers, Smith Elder, recorded their wanderings:

4 June, from Scarborough: 'No letters will find me at Scarborough after the 7th. I do not know where my next address will be. I shall wander a week or two on the East Coast, and only stop at quiet lonely places. No one need be anxious about me as far as I know.'

13 June, from Filey: 'Filey, where we have been for the last week — is a small place with a wild, rocky coast — its sea is very blue — its cliffs are very white — its sands very solitary — it suits Ellen and myself better than Scarborough which is too gay.'

They must certainly have noticed a sharp contrast between the two places. When the York to Scarborough railway opened in 1846 huge numbers of visitors began making for Scarborough, and from being a genteel watering place for the wealthier classes the town suddenly became a booming, bustling seaside resort attracting all manner of visitors from the large Yorkshire industrial towns. There was some justification to the claim that Scarborough was the first of the modern seaside resorts.

Anne Brontë would have known a town of two distinct characters. The salty 'Old Town' of steep, narrow streets and dim alleyways crowded around the harbour, and then rows of fine Georgian and Regency houses spreading out around the South Bay towards the Spa buildings.

Filey was then a small fishing village enjoying a little local fame because of a chalybeate spring, which has long since dried up, somewhere on Carr Naze. Its waters were said to cure apoplexy, epilepsy, asthma and presumably any ailment that a visitor might care to mention!

Charlotte and Ellen lodged at Cliff House with a Mrs Smith. The house, a simple three-storeyed building, can be found on Belle Vue Street, though in Charlotte's time it was known as North Street. Cliff House is now a café-cum-beach shop but there is a sign on a wall, placed there in the Queen's Silver Jubilee Year, to inform visitors of the Brontë connection. The house had been built in 1824 by Mrs Smith's husband. He was a land agent for the Stricklands, a prominent local family who lived at Boynton Hall. Some members of the Smith family are buried in Filey's St Oswald's Church.

When Charlotte and Ellen were at Cliff House they would have enjoyed an unrestricted sea view, no buildings were nearer the sea and the steep fall to the beach was thickly wooded and overgrown with tangled shrubs. Access to the beach was by way of the Coble Landing where the fishing boats still come in.

The view from St. Mary's churchyard, Scarborough, where Anne is buried.

23

Charlotte needed the seclusion of Filey. She would have preferred to stay there for two weeks rather than fall in with Ellen's insistence on going to Easton after just seven days. Her thoughts were turning to home and to Haworth and the strength and courage she would need to carry on. In one of her letters to W S Williams she confided her fears:

'... after I have been a week there (Easton), I intend to return home to Papa. May I retain strength and cheerfulness enough to be a comfort to him and to bear up against the weight of the solitary life to come — it will be solitary — I cannot help dreading the very experience of it.'

Charlotte caught a heavy cold during her days at Easton. She was understandably alarmed and feared for the possible consequences because the first signs of illness with both Emily and Anne had been bouts of painful coughing. It is just possible that she may have had a Burlington doctor recommended to her, a Dr Edward Brett who lived in High Street and had a surgery at the Quay. He was considered to be the foremost doctor in town and would have been known to the Hudson family; it is also possible that he unwittingly helped in the creation of Dr John Graham Bretton, one of the characters in *Villette*.

Charlotte made every effort to conceal her symptoms from Patrick Brontë, but she was to be troubled with soreness of the chest and a persistent cough for the remainder of the year. She spoke of 'that dismal Easton' on her return to Haworth, but her days had not been without activity. Mrs Hudson recalled seeing Charlotte writing every day in the summer house and she may also have been writing while she was in Filey.

Her days in Filey were welcome relief after the long months of sorrow and torment she had endured. In her own way she was relieved and relaxed by the charm and quiet of the little fishing village and absorbed with the abundant natural drama out at sea where waves crashed over the Brigg. She could walk whenever and wherever she wanted and no-one knew or even guessed who she was. It was a time to be alone.

There was also a manuscript to finish and Charlotte clung to her work, fitfully at first, trying to control her grief and keep despair at bay.

In a letter to W S Williams she set out her own therapy: 'Labour must be the cure not sympathy, labour is the only radical cure for rooted sorrow ... Total change might do much ; where that cannot be obtained, work is the best substitute.'

According to Mrs Gaskell, Charlotte's first biographer, she was writing the third and final volume of *Shirley*. Mrs Gaskell believed that Chapter 24, 'The Valley of the Shadow of Death', was the first to be written after Anne's passing.

Charlotte was clearly writing from her own pain :

'With all this care, it seemed strange the sick girl did not get well; yet such was the case: she wasted like any snow-wreath in thaw; she faded like any flower in drought ... and when Mrs Pryor came and quietly demanded a physician, he said she might send for two if she liked. One came, but that one was an oracle: he delivered a dark saying of which the future was to solve the mystery, wrote some prescriptions, gave some directions — the whole with an air of crushing authority — pocketed his fee and went. Probably, he knew well enough he could do no good; but he didn't like to say so.'

Literary critics agree that *Shirley* suffers from breaks in continuity. The character of Caroline Helstone, the heroine, was supposed to have been based physically on Ellen Nussey with much of the emotional nature of Emily, but in the third volume Caroline seems to become more like Anne.

Charlotte eventually returned to Haworth parsonage on 25 June. Emily's dog, Keeper, and Anne's spaniel, Flossy, rushed out to greet her, as if they expected the departed sisters to be not far behind. She let Ellen know of her feelings as she walked into the house :

'I left Papa soon and went into the dining-room. I shut the door. I tried to be glad that I was coming home. I have always been glad before — except once — even then I was cheered, but this time joy was not to be the sensation. I felt that the house was all silent — the rooms were all empty. I remembered where the three were laid — in what narrow dark dwellings — never were they to re-appear on earth. So the sense of desolation and bitterness took possession of me — the agony that was to be undergone — that was not to be avoided, came on ...'

Shirley was published on 26 October, not as successfully as *Jane Eyre*, and criticised for its unevenness and lack of passion, but it did contain some of Charlotte's most vivid writing and some marvellously expressed and richly-varied minor characters.

'Whatever may become of the work the occupation of writing it has been a boon to me. It took me out of a dark and desolate reality into an unreal but happier region.'

Exactly three years later Charlotte would return to the east coast to visit Anne's grave and to spend almost a month alone at Filey. She was writing *Villette* ... but there had been many weeks of restless inactivity.

MAY 1852, FILEY AGAIN

'I am at Filey, utterly alone.'

Charlotte began writing *Villette*, her last and perhaps most accomplished novel, in June, 1851. She worked slowly at first and with little conviction. Sometimes weeks passed with hardly a sentence written.

Charlotte's mind was in a constant turmoil, she slept little, and ill health was a constant strain on her endeavours. At Haworth she led a painfully solitary existence lacking any intellectual companionship, her father was even more of a recluse than he had ever been and there were few visitors to the silent parsonage. Constant reminders of her brother and sisters were everywhere and she could not even bring herself to venture out onto the moors:

'Late in the evening and all through the night I fall into a condition of mind which turns entirely to the past, to memory, and memory is both sad and relentless'.

Visits to London and Edinburgh provided some relief and a measure of enjoyment in spite of her embarrassing shyness. Charlotte stayed in Manchester with Mrs Gaskell and in the Lake District with various acquaintances but she always had to face returning to the gloom and monotony of life at Haworth.

She seemed always to be tired. She had constant headaches, sickness, fever and devastating bouts of depression. Writing was a struggle. In the sorrowful months of 1849 and 1850 Charlotte's work had been her therapy and her hold on life, but now she could not write, she had lost the will.

George Smith, of the publishers Smith, Elder, received a letter in the spring of 1852:

'Expect no good of Currer Bell this summer. For nearly four months now I have not put pen to paper.'

April and May were fruitless months. At the end of May Charlotte went alone to Filey. She had hoped to stay with Miss Wooler at Scarborough but heard from Ellen that Miss Wooler was not going to the coast until late summer. Charlotte again stayed at Cliff House but on this occasion in less expensive rooms. She noticed a number of new lodging houses and the first buildings had appeared on The Crescent, but there were very few visitors so early in the season.

Anne Brontë's grave had to be visited, a task which had pre-occupied

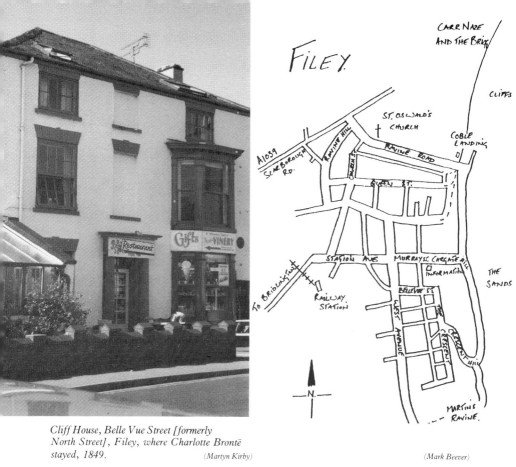

FILEY

Cliff House, Belle Vue Street [formerly North Street], Filey, where Charlotte Brontë stayed, 1849. (Martyn Kirby)

(Mark Beever)

Charlotte for some considerable time. Ellen Nussey had hoped that Charlotte would go with her to Sussex, but Charlotte had declined and had set off for Filey without telling Ellen:

'... long has it lain heavy on my mind — and that was a pilgrimage I felt I could only make alone.'

There were five mistakes on the gravestone, Charlotte left specific instructions for the re-lettering but Anne's headstone still retains one error, her age is given as 28 when it was in fact 29 years. Ellen had registered Anne's death and was responsible for that error.

The weather was quite stormy for the first week, bitterly cold with driving rain. Charlotte had a headache and other ailments and she was feeling the pangs of loneliness, but then the weather improved and the bracing sea air seemed to revitalise her spirits.

In a letter to Miss Wooler Charlotte told of her change of mood:

'I had some dreary evening hours and night-vigils. However, that passed; I think I am now better and stronger from the change, and in a day or two

(Martyn Kirby)

hope to return home. People with my tendency to congestion of the liver — should walk three or four hours every day; accordingly I have walked as much as I could since I came here, and look almost as sunburnt and weather-beaten as a fisherman or a bathing woman with being out in the open air.'

Ellen Nussey received a letter at about the same time:

'Be quite easy about me. I really think I am better for my stay at Filey; that I have derived more benefit from it than I dared to anticipate. I believe, could I stay here two months, and enjoy something like social cheerfulness as well as exercise and good air, my health would be quite renewed.'

References to stormy weather in the many letters Charlotte wrote from Filey at this time are interesting. A mystery letter written by her was discovered in a London bookshop some years after her death. It was addressed to a Miss Ingledew of Southwark, London, and was written from Hartlepool. When Charlotte left Scarborough after Anne's death she had mentioned her intention to 'wander a week or two on the East Coast, and only stop at quiet lonely places' but between leaving Scarborough and arriving at Filey there was little time for her to go up to Hartlepool, whether wandering or using a direct route. She did not mention a Hartlepool address in her letters to W S Williams and, had there been such a visit, Ellen Nussey would have surely mentioned it. Perhaps Charlotte began her holiday in Filey and wandered north during the bad weather, leaving a forwarding address with Mrs Smith.

The letter to Miss Ingledew gives few clues and little information other than Charlotte's opinion of Hartlepool at that time:

'This Hartlepool is a very filthy place indeed and is very badly paved. During the prevalence of the cholera it was inspected by the Health of Towns Commissioner from London, and he said it was the worst place he had ever been in, and it is expected the Town will have to undergo a thorough Cleansing and I can assure you it stands much in need of it. There has been a very heavy storm along the coast here, the sea running mountains high and I am sorry to say attended with great damage to the shipping and loss of life.'

It was signed 'Currer Bell' so Miss Ingledew must have been a literary admirer or someone Charlotte had met in London. Back at Filey Charlotte's many hours of walking included treks out along the cliff paths of Carr Naze to admire the wild splendour of Filey's famous Brigg, or Filey Bridge as it was then known.

The word 'Brigg' is thought to have come from the Scandinavian *Brygja*, meaning a landing place. According to an ancient legend the Devil started to build the Brigg in an attempt to cross the North Sea but he dropped his hammer in the water. When he reached down he picked up a haddock by mistake and the fish still bears his fingerprints.

The Brigg is thought to have inspired a particularly vivid paragraph in Charlotte's novel, *Shirley:*

'A reef of rocks, black and rough, stretches far into the sea; all along, and among, and above these crags, dash and flash, sweep and leap, swells, wreaths, drifts of snowy spray. Some lone wanderer is out on these rocks, treading, with cautious step, the wet, wild sea weed; glancing down into hollows where the brine lies fathoms deep and emerald clear...'

On her very first walk out to the Brigg Charlotte had had to turn back, her progress blocked by two cows ... perhaps for most people a funny incident to look back on, but Charlotte was an unusually small and frail woman and must have been quite frightened.

Charlotte worshipped at St Oswald's parish church above Ravine Road on the way out to Carr Naze Cliffs and the Brigg. A small framed picture on the north wall shows the church as Charlotte would have known it. In the mid-19th century the ravine would have been almost bare of trees; it marked the division between the old East and North Ridings and so the churchyard was over the border. If any Filey resident was near death he or she was said

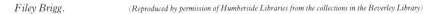

Filey Brigg.

to be 'going over into t' North Riding'. The church has charm and there is an interesting graveyard but the building is of a curious character, and a mixture of styles and intentions are ample evidence of the many efforts at restoration over the centuries.

Methodism had found many converts amongst the Filey fishing families, despite some visiting preachers from Bridlington being pelted with fish! Charlotte wrote to her father: 'There is a well meaning but utterly inactive clergyman at Filey, and methodists flourish.' The clergyman was Thomas Norfolk Jackson and he was the vicar of Filey for a total of 40 years. Charlotte's observations were entirely accurate, St Oswald's was apparently held together by plaster and whitewash, congregations were small and the church seemed to have been run in a very careless manner. Items of silver plate disappeared without explanation, the church registers were often mislaid and no one seemed to be unduly concerned.

Charlotte described the church and a strange incident which amused her so much that she wanted to share it:

'It was certainly not more than thrice the length and breadth of our passage, floored with brick, the walls green with mould, the pews painted white, but the paint almost off with time and decay.

'At one end there is a little gallery for the singers, and when these personages stood up to perform, they all turned their backs upon the congregation, and the congregation turned their backs upon pulpit and parson. The effect of this manoeuvre was so ludicrous I could hardly help laughing ; had Mr Nicholls been there he certainly would have laughed out.'

Needless to say the church furniture is now arranged in the more usual pattern and Sunday services are conducted with dignity! Charlotte may also have seen sheep in the church. It was quite a normal occurrence because much of the floor was bricked and the sheep were encouraged to keep down the grass and weeds growing between the stones.

The weeks at Filey were a tonic. Charlotte was refreshed and rested and her health was much improved but there was still *Villette* to finish and she had again to face the emptiness and anxieties of life at the parsonage.

She wrote to W S Williams after her return home:

'The warm weather and a visit to the sea have done me much good physically; but as yet I have recovered neither elasticity of animal spirits, nor flow of the power of composition. And if it were otherwise, the difference would be of no avail ; my time and thoughts are at present taken up with close attendance on my father, whose health is just now in a very critical state ...'

Patrick Brontë had suffered a stroke and needed nursing and Charlotte's own health was beginning to suffer. She resolved to complete *Villette* as soon as possible and informed her friends, as politely as possible, that no visitors would be encouraged until her work was completed. She refused an invitation to visit George Smith and his wife in London and worked on through the remaining summer weeks. The story of *Villette* was making enormous demands on Charlotte's emotions and experience, her health began to suffer and she was feeling the constant weight and strain of loneliness.

A letter to Ellen Nussey in August revealed much of Charlotte's thinking; she had nothing to look forward to, her future was to be bleak and inevitably sad:

'I am silent because I have literally nothing to say. I might indeed repeat over and over again that my life is a pale blank and often a very weary burden, and that the future sometimes appals me; but what end would be answered by such repetition except to weary you and enervate myself.

'The evils that now and then wring a groan from my heart, lie in position, not that I am a single woman and likely to remain a single woman, but because I am a lonely woman and likely to be lonely. But it cannot be helped and therefore imperatively must be borne ...'

Ellen Nussey was allowed to stay at the parsonage for a week in early October and her companionship must have restored some of Charlotte's vigour because the first two volumes of *Villette* were completed by the end of the month, the third and final volume was at the publishers' by the end of November and *Villette* was in the bookshops in January, 1853. Charlotte had endured a protracted and worrying silence from her publishers before they acknowledged receipt of the manuscript. She was even considering setting off for London to find out just what was happening when the longed-for letter from Smith, Elder finally arrived. It was very favourable. Charlotte's book was, to use Mrs Gaskell's phrase, 'received with one burst of acclamation'.

Villette is the story of Lucy Snowe, a plain English girl without family or friends who goes to Brussels to teach at a girls' school. There she meets John Bretton, a handsome young English doctor, but instead of falling for him, as would be expected from any other lady novelist of that generation, she becomes increasingly fascinated with M Paul Emanuel, a much older man. He is a prickly-tempered but golden-hearted professor who, of course, mellows in later chapters. He sets Lucy up as headteacher of her own school but then circumstances part the pair and the reader is left to wonder whether they will ever see each other again.

Charlotte had drawn on her experiences in Brussels. She had gone there with Emily in 1842 to attend the Pensionnat Heger, a school for young ladies, as pupil teachers, the intention being that the sisters would improve their foreign languages, and any qualifications they might gain would help them when they eventually set up their own school.

At the Pensionnat Charlotte came under the spell of M Constantin Heger, husband of the owner, a mature academic with a magnetic personality. She fell deeply in love with him, but her affection was only returned with a guarded politeness. They corresponded but Charlotte stopped writing when M Heger asked that letters for him should no longer be sent to the Pensionnat but to another school where he taught.

Charlotte had tried to deal with her feelings for M Heger in her very first novel, *The Professor*, but the manuscript was rejected at least seven times by various publishers. Indeed at one time Charlotte had suggested to George Smith that he really should use the pages for lighting cigars!

In *Villette* what is essentially the same theme, that of a master-pupil love affair, is handled with the scope and power of a writer at the very height of her powers. The thoughts had come slowly because she was writing from pained experience and reviving suppressed emotions, but when the book was published it left a number of influential critics regretting the instant fame of *Jane Eyre*, for they believed *Villette* to be Charlotte's finest work.

She had visited London in January of the New Year to supervise the proof corrections of *Villette* but that reason may have been just an excuse to get away from Haworth. On the thirteenth day of December Mr Nicholls, her father's Irish curate, had both surprised and shocked Charlotte by proposing marriage and when Patrick Brontë had found out he had worked himself into a fit of uncontrollable anger. Mr Nicholls offered to resign his curacy, but made no move to leave Haworth.

'He entered — he stood before me. What his words were you can guess; his manner — you can hardly realize — never can I forget it. Shaking from head to foot, looking deadly pale, speaking low, vehemently yet with difficulty — he made me for the first time feel what it costs a man to declare affection where he doubts response. The spectacle of one ordinarily so statue-like, thus trembling, stirred, and overcome, gave me a kind of strange shock.'

In the year 1853 there was so much tension at the parsonage that Charlotte would be away as often as was possible.

The Crescent, Filey. (*Reproduced by permission of Humberside Libraries from the collections in the Beverley Library*)

Section four

HORNSEA, SEPTEMBER 1853

'A happy and pleasant week'

During the late summer of 1853 Charlotte visited the Yorkshire coast for the last time, staying with her dear friend and former teacher, Miss Margaret Wooler at Hornsea.

There were many other opportunities for travel during the year. Charlotte's trip to London had been timely because the tension and open hostility between Charlotte's father and Mr Nicholls had made life at the parsonage almost unbearable for her. When she returned to Haworth Charlotte had so dreaded the moment of entering her own home that she had pleaded with Ellen Nussey to meet the train at Keighley and accompany her. Mr Brontë's attitude and temper had not changed and Nicholls would only enter the parsonage if his business was absolutely essential.

Arthur Bell Nicholls had seemed the unlikeliest suitor. Charlotte had been shocked and surprised by his initial declarations but she had handled him with considerable sympathy. Patrick Brontë was adamant that his daughter deserved a better prospect and even the Brontë servants, John and Martha Brown, treated Nicholls with ill-disguised contempt. Nicholls had neither wealth nor position and both father and daughter shared the opinion that the taciturn curate was not even her intellectual equal:

'I pity him but I don't like that dark gloom of his. He dogged me up the lane after the evening service in no pleasant manner, he stopped also in the passage after the Bishop and the other clergy were gone into the room, and it was because I drew away and went upstairs that he gave that look which filled Martha's soul with horror ... If Mr Nicholls be a good man at bottom, it is a sad thing that nature has not given him the faculty to put goodness into a more attractive form.'

Yet she gradually warmed to him. Nicholls had made his feelings known at an anxious time in Charlotte's life. She had completed *Villette* but the task had certainly exhausted her creative energy and many biographers have wondered whether, married or not, she would have ever written anything of real quality again.

The visit to London had more than ever convinced Charlotte that life in literary and fashionable circles was far too hectic and intense for her. She was obviously ill-equipped for meeting new people, she shrank from public gaze, her conversation was limited, she had almost no appreciation of

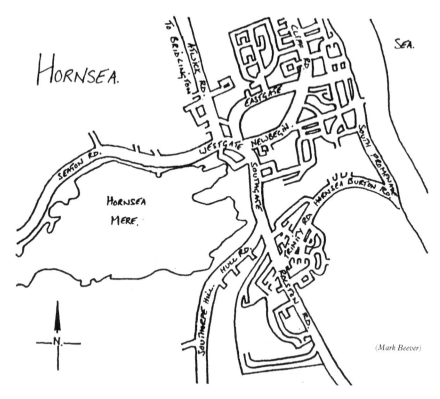

HORNSEA.

(Mark Beever)

humour and even the comings and goings and moderate excitements of a short stay in Manchester with Mrs Gaskell were enough to depress her.

At her Haworth home she spoke to no-one but the servants for weeks on end and she had become used to such isolation over the years; the postman's arrival was an event to anticipate, the most exciting moment of the day. Charlotte endured her existence, she did not possess the character or personality to enjoy a fuller life.

Mr Nicholls could not face the uncertainty of Charlotte's feelings and he could no longer work with her ill-tempered father so he went ahead with his resignation and became curate at Kirk Smeaton, near Pontefract. He wrote in guarded tones to Charlotte and she replied. Many months later he stayed with a friend in Oxenhope and Charlotte walked there to meet him, but their communications were secret.

Charlotte's health suffered again during the early summer months. She blamed influenza but again the loneliness of her life and the heavy depression she could soon sink into must have contributed to her low spirits. Mrs Gaskell had hoped to visit Haworth during the summer but she had to wait until September. Patrick Brontë's health had fluctuated, perhaps in keeping with his moods. Charlotte had long hoped to be able to visit Miss Wooler, who was staying in Hornsea for the summer, but her plans had to be postponed a number of times.

In August she wrote to Miss Wooler: 'All the summer I felt the wish and cherished the intention to join you for a brief period at the seaside, nor do I yet relinquish the purpose, though its fulfilment must depend on my father's health.' — A week later she wrote again, 'My prospects, however, of being able to leave home continue unsettled.'

By September Mr Brontë's health and disposition were much better and Charlotte felt able to leave him for a week.

Hornsea was much smaller than the other resorts Charlotte had visited. It enjoyed some fame as a spa town before the railway link was completed in 1864, and was popular with well-to-do Hull families. A Hull doctor described the town's spring waters as an 'excellent tonic' and Dr Granville, in his *Spas of England*, praised the quality of the sea water. Hornsea was a very quiet and dignified town and its prime attractions were the 467-acre mere, the largest freshwater lake in Yorkshire, and wide sweeping beaches. There was sufficient for Charlotte. She walked on the sands and the long rambling paths around the mere enjoying the companionship of her dear old friend.

Charlotte had enjoyed a deep and lasting friendship with Miss Wooler. Charlotte's days at Roe Head School had not been altogether happy and there had been difficulties but when she was a pupil teacher the friendship grew into something rather special. A quotation from Mrs Gaskell's biography is worthy of note:

'Though the duties of the day might be tedious and monotonous, there were always two or three happy hours to look forward to in the evening, when she and Miss Wooler sat together — sometimes late into the night — and had quiet pleasant conversations, or pauses of silence as agreeable, because each felt that as soon as a thought or remark occurred which they wished to express, there was an intelligent companion ready to sympathise, and yet they were not compelled to "make talk".'

Miss Wooler had taken rooms at 94 Newbegin, a main thoroughfare leading from the town centre Market Place to the distant sea shore. It was one of six houses in a terraced row built to cater specifically for holidaymakers. The floor to ceiling windows on the second storey are evidence of a balcony which was there in Charlotte's day; the exterior walls are now concrete-rendered but were once stucco. At the time of writing number 94, which Charlotte would have known as 4 Swiss Terrace, was being sympathetically restored to make it as near the original as possible. The original doors, wooden fittings and fireplace were receiving much care and attention and there was talk of rebuilding the balcony eventually.

Charlotte returned to Haworth in a much happier frame of mind and wrote to Miss Wooler: 'The week I spent at Hornsea was a happy and pleasant week. Thank you, my dear Miss Wooler — for the true kindness which gave it its chief charm. I shall think of you often, especially when I walk out — and during the long evenings. I believe the weather has at length taken a turn; today is beautifully fine. I wish I were at Hornsea and just now preparing to go out with you to walk on the sands or along the lake.'

She recounted an incident on the return journey which began when a respectable looking woman and her child hailed the coach halfway between Hornsea and Hull:

'The child took her place opposite me; she had not sat long before — without any previous warning, or the slightest complaint of nausea — sickness seized her and the contents of her little stomach — consisting apparently of a milk breakfast — were unceremoniously deposited in my lap! Of course I alighted from the coach in a pretty mess, but succeeded in procuring water and a towel at the station with which I managed to make my dress and cloak once more presentable.'

Mrs Gaskell came to Haworth later the same month and there was a noticeable change in Mr Brontë's attitude to Nicholls. Haworth's new curate, Rev George de Renzi, had hardly come up to expectations and Brontë was beginning to realise the true worth of Mr Nicholls.

Charlotte's patience was succeeding. She wrote to Ellen in April: 'Papa's consent is gained — in fact dear Ellen I am engaged!'

Ellen Nussey was uneasy about the relationship, suspecting that Nicholls would discourage her friendship with Charlotte. Mrs Gaskell feared that the

94 Newbegin [formerly 4 Swiss Terrace], Hornsea, where Charlotte Brontë stayed, 1853, in the house 4th from left, largely obscured by the tree. (Neil Fleming)

marriage would put an end to Charlotte's writing and even Charlotte admitted to having certain misgivings, but the wedding went ahead on 29 June, 1854. Only Ellen Nussey and Miss Margaret Wooler were present. Patrick Brontë had suddenly announced that he would not attend the ceremony — illness was his excuse — so Miss Wooler was asked to give her former pupil away.

The honeymoon was spent in Ireland where Charlotte would meet some of her husband's relatives. She and Nicholls journeyed to Conway and Bangor in North Wales and then crossed the sea to visit Dublin, Cork and Killarney. On the west coast they stayed at Kilkee, a small fishing village.

'Such a wild, iron bound coast — with such an ocean view as I had not yet seen and such battling of waves with rocks as I had never imagined.'

There Charlotte and Nicholls walked out onto the cliff tops to admire the breaking waves. She wanted to be alone and she wanted quiet, and Nicholls complied without a murmur: 'The first morning we went out on to the cliffs and saw the Atlantic coming in all white foam, I did not know whether I should get leave or time to take the matter in my own way. I did not want to talk — but I did want to look and be silent. Having hinted a petition, licence was not refused — covered with a rug to keep off the spray I was allowed to sit where I chose — and he only interrupted me when he thought I crept too near the edge of the cliff. So far he is always good in this way ...'

He was no Rochester and no Paul Emanuel, he was probably dull and an uninteresting talker but he made Charlotte far happier than she had expected:

'I find my husband the tenderest nurse, the kindest support — the best earthly comfort ever woman had.'

But Charlotte's joy was to be shortlived. After a long walk with her husband on the moors she caught a cold and could not shake it off. The first stages of pregnancy weakened her already frail constitution and, after being encouraged to take yet another very long walk, amazingly enough in wet grass and with thin shoes, she was laid low. A fever developed and she gradually worsened.

Death came on the last day of March, 1855:

'Oh! I am not going to die, am I? He will not separate us, we have been so happy.'

It is difficult to conceive of a sadder life.

Charlotte Brontë knew almost unrelieved and wearisome sadness. She lived in a cold, bleak house overlooking a poverty-stricken Pennine village now prettified beyond belief but in her day gloomy, dreary and appallingly unhealthy.

The only attraction of home was the love and intimate companionship of Emily and Branwell and, to a slightly lesser degree, her younger sister, Anne. When they were gone Charlotte was left empty and alone until her brief, happy months of marriage. Her visits to the Yorkshire coast came at times in her life when a complete change of mood and surroundings was absolutely essential to her well-being. She loved the sea, adored the freshness of the landscape and gloried in the wild excitement and constant drama of breaking waves and skidding clouds.

Had her circumstances been any different Charlotte Brontë would have chosen to live in a cliff-top cottage somewhere on the Yorkshire coast.

She would certainly have been much happier.

Infants School, Hornsea c.1848
(Reproduced by permission of Humberside Libraries from the collections in the Beverley Library)

CHARLOTTE BRONTË — A CHRONOLOGY

1811 — Patrick Brontë appointed curate at Hartshead-cum-Clifton, Yorkshire.

1815 — Mr Brontë moves to Thornton, Bradford.

1816 — Charlotte born Thursday, 21 April at Thornton.
Older sisters, Maria and Elizabeth, were born at Hartshead.
Branwell, Emily and Anne were born at Thornton.

1820 — February: The family moves to Haworth.

1821 — September: Mrs Brontë dies. Her sister, Elizabeth Branwell, takes charge of the family.

1824 — August: Charlotte goes to Cowan Bridge School, Maria and Elizabeth are already there, Emily joins them later.

1825 — Maria (May) and Elizabeth (June) sicken and die.
Emily and Charlotte are taken home.

1831 — January: Charlotte goes to Miss Wooler's School at Roe Head, near Dewsbury; she meets and befriends Ellen Nussey and Mary Taylor.

1832 — July: Charlotte leaves Roe Head School.

1835 — July: Charlotte returns to Roe Head as a governess/teacher.

1838 — May: She leaves Roe Head.

1839 — May: Charlotte becomes governess to the Sidgwick Family of Stonegappe Hall, Lothersdale.
July: She leaves.
September: Charlotte and Ellen Nussey go to BRIDLINGTON , staying with Mr and Mrs Hudson at Easton.

1842 — February: Patrick Brontë accompanies Charlotte and Emily to Brussels where they enrol at the Pensionnat Heger.
October: Aunt Branwell dies; Charlotte and Emily return to Haworth.

1843 — January: Charlotte returns to Brussels on her own; she stays until the following January.

1844 — August: Arthur Nicholls appointed curate at Haworth.

1847 — October: *Jane Eyre* is published.

1848 — 24 September: Branwell dies.
19 December: Emily dies.

1849 — 28 May: Anne dies at SCARBOROUGH. Charlotte is with her.
Charlotte spends some time in FILEY and revisits the Hudsons at Easton.
October: *Shirley* is published.

1852 — June: Charlotte is writing *Villette*. She goes alone to FILEY and visits Anne's grave at SCARBOROUGH.
December: Rev Arthur Nicholls proposes marriage to Charlotte.
1853 — January: *Villette* is published.
September: Charlotte stays with Miss Wooler at HORNSEA.
1854 — 29 June: Charlotte and Nicholls are married.
1855 — 31 March : Charlotte dies aged 38 years.
1857 — Mrs Gaskell's *Life of Charlotte Brontë* is published.

Bridlington, 1848.
(*Reproduced by permission of Humberside Libraries from the collections in the Beverley Library*)